The pain
you feel
today, will
be the
strength you
feel
tomorrow.

ROGUE

REP
B3X
1st PLAC

AGAIN FASTER
EQUIPMENT

Calvin Klein

Calvin Klein

ROGUE
35

VIRUS

1:19

2XU

FOUR CALIBER

ROGUE
ROGUE

CPSIA information can be obtained
at www.ICGtesting.com
Printed in the USA
BVHW020000070319
541824BV00045B/232/P

9 780368 364914